The Relationship Chronicles

Straight Talk, Real Love, No Drama!

Judi Mason

DIVA Ink Publishers
Atlanta, Georgia

The Relationship Chronicles
Copyright © 2012 Judi Mason

For further information please contact:
Judi Mason by visiting www.judimason.com
or write to the office of Judi Mason

P.O. Box 7394
Atlanta, GA 30357
Email: info@judimason.com

Layout & Design: Susan L. Volkert
Editing: Scott Roberts
Published by: DIVA Ink

Library of Congress Control Number: 2012943552
Printed in the United States of America
ISBN:978-0-9858625-0-3

All rights are reserved. No part of this publication may be reproduced or transmitted in any form or by any means, electronic or mechanical, including photocopying, recording or by any information storage and retrieval system, without the prior written permission of the author, except for the inclusion of brief quotations in a review.

Contents

Foreword, ix
Relationship Tune-Up, 1
Men Versus Women: Is There Really a Battle of the Sexes?, 7
How to Handle Selfish People, 13
What Women Really Want, 17
Have You Heard the Silent Screams of Those You Love?, 23
Courage to Love, 27
Does Your Man Hear You When You Speak?, 33
Can We Find Love Together?, 39
Are You Giving Your Haters Too Much Credit?, 45
Are You Destroying Your Relationships?, 49
Emotional Healing Is a Step Away, 53
Spread the Love, 57
Your Pride Will Humble You, 61
Where Is the Love for Your Friends?, 65
Mind Your Own Business, 69
Love and Encouragement Challenge, 73
Finding Love Outside the Box, 77
Prescription for Mental Peace, 83
Settling Is Not an Option, 89
Are You Choosing Wisely?, 97
Are You Guilty of the "Just In Case", 103
Bring Closure to a Dead Relationship, 109
Chloe Mantra, 115

Foreword

When I sat down to write *The Chloe Chronicles: Life Lesson's I Learned From My Cocker Spaniel*, the first installment of The Chronicle book series, I knew that this series would be special because it focused on the best product ever created: YOU! When I was in a place of needing a personal overall I was bombarded with so much that I couldn't see the forest for the trees, so I began to design my own plan of becoming my best self. I have had such success with the program personally and with my clients that I thought that I would share it with the masses. There are three core elements involved in becoming your best self:

Rediscovering:
A journey of self discovery—*The Chloe Chronicles*
Reconnecting:
Defining your true desires—*The Relationship Chronicles*
Reinventing:
Life application—*The Best Self Chronicles*

As you can see, each phase has a corresponding book in the Chronicle series that helps bring a portion of each element to life. I am a firm believer that we have one life and that we should live it to the fullest, and the Chronicles series allows you to do just that. It helps you discover your true desires in life, love, and relationships and then shows you how to implement them. Recognizing that each person is uniquely different, the series cites key examples to use as a guide to help you reach your goals. In a time when the cares of life are overwhelming and people are losing their jobs in record numbers, their self-identity is loss and they can't see past their immediate needs to reconnect with their hearts' desires. The Chronicle series helps individuals begin the discovery process of reconnecting with themselves. Each book is filled with an array of real-life principles and testimonials of real-life application that will help the reader develop and implement changes in their own lives.

I can't thank you enough for the positive feedback and support of *The Chloe Chronicles*; it really helps affirm that I was on the right track. I am so excited to now introduce you to the second installment, *The Relationship Chronicles: Straight Talk, Real Love, No Drama!* I know it will be just as helpful in this key area of life.

For almost two years, I was a featured author for an online magazine with a weekly column that focused on life, love, and relationships from a spiritual perspective. Weekly I would write from my experiences and, most of all, from my heart to help spare others from the mistakes that I endured, and to hopefully put them on a journey to fostering healthy relationships. A lot of my articles challenged the reader to a level of accountability and action. In an effort to soften the blow, I would always end my articles with an endearing remark such as with love. I received so many emails regarding my most popular articles, I decided to put them together in a compilation and *The Relationship Chronicles: Straight Talk, Real Love, No Drama!* was born.

In *The Relationship Chronicles*, I share real life situations that will hopefully help you look at your relationships from a different point of view and foster communication regarding needs and boundaries. I believe that we are empowered to empower others, and I hope my mistakes and encounters will help you grow and thrive in every area of your life. May The Relationship Chronicles begin your journey to authentic and successful relationships.

Here's to our growth! You are not alone; I am on the same journey too!

Judi

Love Yourself

Friendship with ones self is all important, because without it one cannot be friends with anyone else in the world.
—Eleanor Roosevelt

Be True to Yourself

"Living with integrity means: Not settling for less than what you know you deserve in your relationships. Asking for what you want and need from others. Speaking your truth, even though it might create conflict or tension. Behaving in ways that are in harmony with your personal values. Making choices based on what you believe, and not what others believe."
—Barbara De Angelis

*L*IFE IS FULL OF SURPRISES and no matter which way you turn, there are new experiences awaiting you around every corner. Each experience comes with a lesson and if the lesson isn't learned, you will encounter similar experiences until the hidden message is revealed. Relationships are no different. They are often tricky because you have two people with their own unspoken needs and expectations coming together to forge a bond. Unfortunately we are not given a handbook on how to have successful relationships, so we typically base our decisions on personal experiences, good and bad; in doing so we inadvertently continue to make unhealthy choices that sabotage our relationships.

We all have been disappointed and have made major mistakes, but we have to take time and learn from those mistakes and make the necessary changes if we want to cultivate healthy, authentic relationships. If we don't, we will continually fail in this area of our lives. I believe that a lot of disappointment in relationships has a lot to do with setting unrealistic expectations on people who are clueless to your relational needs. Have you communicated your relational needs and boundaries? Do you even know what they are?

Maybe it's time to evaluate your relationships:

- Have you ever taken the time to really ask yourself, what do I want in my relationships-platonic or intimate?
- Are you being treated the way you want to be treated?
- Do you have realistic expectations of others and yourself?
- Are you being the friend to others that you desire them to be to you?
- If people treated you the way that you treated them (especially when they are not around) would you be pleased?

In order to have authentic relationships, we have to be honest with ourselves. Take time today to perform a relationship check. Write a list of your relationship desires, deal breakers, and expectations and see if your current relationships are measuring up to your standards. If they are, GREAT! If not, it's time to make some changes starting with you. If your relationships are not where you want them to be, what changes can be made to reach that desired goal? Have you communicated your desires? If not, let your friends know what your wants and needs are in a relationship and see if you can reach a happy medium.

There is a quote by Mother Teresa that I love: **Let no one ever come to you without leaving better and happier.** If we are not better for having been with each other, why are we together? We have to choose to live on purpose and in doing so, value the relationships that are put in our lives. Really assess if your current relationships are right for you. Choose not to just have people around you, but choose to have purposeful relationships that require you to go higher and become your best self.

Much love,

Judi

Men Versus Women: Is There Really a Battle of the Sexes?

When it comes to relationships, it seems like a battle or a conflict is taking place between men and women. Each gender has very diverse ideas in regards to what a relationship should look like, let alone be like. The battle of the sexes is the constant struggle of men and women trying to gain a mutual understanding of one another.

In an effort to bridge the gap, I interviewed a number of men and women between the ages of 25-55 concerning the top five things that they want the opposite sex to know regarding relationships. As you can imagine, each side had a variety of opinions.

Top five things women want men to know from a woman's perspective:

1. **Communicate more.** When a problem arises or you are confronted about issues, don't run away and hide. Face the problem and work it out like an adult.
2. **Be Honest.** If you don't want a committed relationship and you just want to play the field, then articulate that fact. Stop involving women in a "committed" relationship when you have no desire to be monogamous.
3. **Get a job.** It is not a woman's responsibility to take care

of a man. A man should take care of himself.

4. **Chivalry is not dead.** A woman would like to see a man take the lead, take the initiative; open a door, pull out a chair, hold an umbrella over her in the rain, etc. Treat her like the lady that she is.

5. **Every woman isn't attracted to you.** Don't try to date every woman you meet. Appreciate and respect the women that God sends into your life. Some women were meant to just be your friend. Cherish that friendship.

Top five things men want women to know from a man's perspective:

1. **Respect yourself.** Be a lady. Carry yourself in a more dignified manner. Stop wearing such revealing clothes. Leave a little something to the imagination.

2. **Know your value and your worth.** Stop settling for less. Demand more; expect more and you will get more.

3. **Guard your heart.** Stop giving men your heart, especially when they haven't earned it.

4. **Friends first.** Enjoy the friendship phase of the relationship. Don't rush pass that phase to get to something more serious.

5. **Do you!** Stop allowing your man's needs, wants, and desires to overshadow your own. Stay focused on your dreams, aspirations, and goals. The rest will follow, including your man.

It is amazing how the issues are not remotely similar between the sexes. It just continues to highlight the differences between men and women, even to the core of what's tolerated and what is expected. Instead of automatically being pro or con, I listened to their answers and allowed myself to really think about the points that were being made. Subconsciously, I began internally examining myself, asking if I am guilty of any of these charges. Be it male or female, I believe that we all could work on one thing on the list.

As always, I hope these tips have offered you some insight.

Much love,

Judi

How to
Handle
Selfish
People

My two-second vent on selfish people: Selfish people cause grief in the lives that they touch. They have no regard for others. They are counterfeit individuals: fake, phony, frauds who take up space in your life. They are not in **any** relationship to give; they are in them to **take. Selfish, self-centered people are nothing but a distraction.**

After dealing with people who use and manipulate others and take their kindness for weakness out of a selfish motive, I was ready to really expound on this subject. I was prepared to give my high-minded speech on selfish, self-centered people. Believe me, I had a lot to say. And then I was stopped dead in my tracks. While channel surfing, I heard a sermon that sounded like God was speaking directly to me. The minister said:

- What is your motivation for helping others?
- Why do you do what you do for others?
- Is it out of your own desires?
- Is it out of a desire to please God and give Him glory?

He explained that if you operate out of your own desire and you are hurt and offended then that is your fault. But if you operate out of a desire to please God and to bring God glory, then no one can hurt you. God has you and what you do for someone else, God will make happen for you. Don't be discouraged; God will honor your commitment. Needless to say, after that reality check, my perspective changed. After hearing that, I wrote the following prayer:

Lord, give me the wisdom and foresight to recognize the counterfeits and distractions in my life and the ability to handle them accordingly.

I think if we are able to recognize those who are counterfeits and distractions, we will not get caught in the drama of people who are not supposed to be in our lives in the first place. Examine those around you and ask God why they are in your life. Remember, some people are in your life for a second, a moment, and some are there for a lifetime. Don't make the mistake of making someone who is temporary permanent.

Be encouraged. Allow the Lord to heal any pain, grief, or discomfort caused by selfish individuals.

Walk in your victory! Remember, we win!

With love,

Judi

What Women Really Want

I HAD THE PLEASURE OF WATCHING THE MOVIE *ROBIN HOOD*, starring Russell Crowe. In the movie, the men were off to war for 10 years and the women were left caring for the villages, tending the fields, fending off the poachers, and making the best of a bad situation. When the men returned, life returned. The people were happy. The fields were tended and the villages were protected. At that moment, it reminded me of what a difference a man makes.

Men, if you never hear this from another woman, let me say, **WE NEED YOU.** Yes, we can do it without you because some women have been placed in that position; but that is not the way God intended it to be. The balance that you bring to the table, the security that you represent, the weight that you carry as the provider, and the love that you give when you really give your all is irreplaceable. That is worth more than gold.

Men often state that women are complicated and at times, we can be, but we really aren't that complex when it comes to what we really want from a man.

What women want is really simple:

- We want to be loved.
- We want to be shown love and appreciation. Flowers and gifts are great, but we want to hear you tell us

"I love you, thank you, and I appreciate you." That means so much more.

- We want you to have a listening ear when we talk to you because in our minds, you are our best friend.
- We try to respect your space, but in doing so, we feel neglected and taken for granted. At those times, just take a moment and reassure us.
- We want you to make an effort and try (even when you don't want to) to help and be the partner in the relationship that you promised you would be—the friend, the lover, the support.
- We want you to keep your word and do what you said you were going to do. We aren't nagging you; we just want you to follow through with your promises.
- But most importantly, at the end of it all, what we really want is YOU.

Several years ago, the man in my life gave me everything; the provision, the encouragement, the support, the friendship, the communication, and the security that I desired. In essence, I had it all; except him. Due to issues in his childhood, he put up an emotional block and never gave of himself but he gave everything else. His way of showing that he cared was to give *things*. He had protected himself for so long that when he wanted to give his all, he didn't know how. Years later it became such a struggle that he finally realized how emotionally handicapped he had become.

It took a while for me to realize and truly understand that he indeed loved me, and the love he showed me was the best he could give. However, in my mind, I could not comprehend his love because, for me, love equated to having the person—the man— not the stuff. And at the end of it all, he was unable to give me what I really wanted—himself.

Most men want to be the provider and protector, and we love that. But in doing so, be sure to give us what we really want: YOU—the good, the bad and the indifferent. Don't be ashamed of your scars; we have them too. Don't be ashamed of being vulnerable; we are vulnerable too. Don't be ashamed to be afraid; we are afraid too.

Allow us to walk throughout this journey called life together. And in doing so, we will make mistakes, we will miss the mark, and we will eventually get it right, but let's get it right together. We love you and we need you. Allow yourself to love us, the way we really need to be loved, by giving us all of you.

Know that this was written in love,

Judi

Have You Heard the Silent Screams of Those You Love?

MANY INDIVIDUALS ARE SO FOCUSED ON BEING IN LOVE that they don't take time to get to know the REAL person that they are in love with—their good, their past and their issues. People are married, engaged, and dating total strangers, and they don't even know it. Be sure that you take the time to sit down and find out about the real person who you are involved with. Do you know their struggles? Do you know their pain? Do you know their past? Do you really know them?

On November 5, 2010, *The Oprah Winfrey Show* aired an episode dedicated to men who had been molested. On the show, writer-director Tyler Perry joined Oprah and an audience of 200 men who were victims of molestation. The show opened with the men standing, holding a picture of themselves at the age that they were first molested. For some, this would be the first time that they would share their stories. As you can imagine, the stories of the abuse were graphic and horrific. The tales of how their innocence was lost is heartbreaking. No one should have to endure ANY abuse, especially not an innocent child. Although this show was dedicated to men, women have suffered as well. I beg of each of you, take this opportunity to really connect with those who you love, reach out to them and let them know that you are there for them. Open the line of communication regarding this topic and others and provide them with a loving, empathetic, non-judgmental safe place where they can share their encounter. Offer them the trust, confidentiality, support, love, and friendship that they need and deserve. Don't try to have all the answers, because sometimes you won't. But provide them with what you do have and that is LOVE and comfort.

If you or someone you know has been abused, the following link offers information on available resources: http://www.oprah.com/packages/sexual-abuse-resource-center.html

In addition to counseling, sometimes people just need prayer. Here are two prayer lines that can offer prayer support as well:

Kenneth Copeland Prayer Line (817-852-6000)
(available 24 hours a day, seven days a week)

Joyce Meyers Prayer Line (1-866-349-3300)
(available Monday-Friday 7 pm-4 am CST)

My prayer is that this will begin to open the lines of communication that will foster genuine relationships and offer the support that will set individuals free.

May the love of God surround you!

Much love,

Judi

Over the past few months, I have encountered several men and women who are fearful of accepting the love of others. Life, bad relationships, negative thought patterns coupled with disappointments one right after the other have really taken a toll on a lot of people. Some people will never know because they wear the "Everything is okay with me" mask on a daily basis. People are no longer authentic and transparent, which allows pain and hurt to overtake them to such a degree that when TRUE blessings come, they are not in a position to receive them.

Everyone is looking for love—love of a friend, love from family, love of a spouse—and when true genuine love comes, you know it. However, when that true love comes, are you ready for it? Many have allowed counterfeit associates and "friends" to dumb down and numb them to the reality of true genuine Godly love from one human being to another. Many have become so accustomed to disappointment that they sabotage the relationships that God sends, because they have lost faith in a genuine relationship being a reality in their lives.

Out of fear, people are holding onto their pride and not allowing themselves to be vulnerable and receive the love that they truly deserve. The main reason is in the past, they shared their heart with the wrong people, those who were not worthy of their love. Now when the right one comes along, they are so in bondage to the prideful declaration that, "No one is ever going to hurt me again", they miss the blessing that God has for them.

Both men and women are equally as guilty of not allowing themselves to be open and vulnerable to another human being. Instead they let fear destroy a genuine relationship in order to maintain a phony one. Unfortunately, at the end of the day, regret sets in and they realize they let a blessing from God go due to their own insecurities.

Today, choose to let go of your pain from the past. Forgive anyone who hurt you; release them so that you can free yourself. Allow God to heal you and bless you the way that HE wants to bless you. And receive the REAL love that can only come from Him. Remember, you have a part to play, too, so choose wisely.

Choose to: Love earnestly! Live life to the fullest! Live with no regrets!

Enjoy the real love that you truly deserve!

Much love,

Judi

P.S. Here is the best picture of what true love looks like.

- Love is patient and kind.
- Love is not jealous or boastful or proud or rude.
- It does not demand its own way.
- It is not irritable, and it keeps no record of being wronged.
- It does not rejoice about injustice but rejoices whenever the truth wins out.
- Love never gives up, never loses faith, is always hopeful, and endures through every circumstance.

1 Corinthians 13:4-7 (NLT)

Does Your Man Hear You When You Speak?

SEVERAL YEARS AGO, I thought about writing a book entitled *How to Effectively Communicate with Your Man*. At the time, it seemed like communication in relationships was a hot topic. Of course I was very open to the topic because at the time, I was having a very hard time effectively communicating with the man in my life. I felt like we were speaking two different languages and neither one of us felt the need to take the time to attempt to learn the other person's communication style. In order to move forward in the relationship, we decided to work on the way we communicated by acknowledging the problems in our individual communication skills.

Below are twelve tidbits that I learned during my time of communication discovery. I don't believe that all men are the same. But I do believe that they possess similar foundational characteristics that aid in the application of these tidbits.

Personally I believe that majority of these skills could be used with women as well. By no means do I claim to be a communications expert, but I have lived on both sides of the communication spectrum and there is nothing better than the effective communication side. I hope these tidbits help.

12 Ways to effectively communicate with your man:

- **Speak in headlines.** Women are too detail-oriented. Men really don't care what you have to say. They love you, but they don't want to hear every detail. Give them the short, short version—10 seconds or less. Speak in prases as if you were reading the headlines in the newspaper to him. Then he will hear you. (Trust me on this one, ladies.)
- **Know your man.** You know your man's temperment, his likes and dislikes, and you also know his pain points. You know how to love him and you know how to make him bleed. At all times, use wisdom and walk in love in every area. However, when angry, be very careful in your decision to inflict pain. Men are much more sensitive than you think and if you draw blood too often, you might eventually reach a point of no return.
- **Set your expectations.** This depends on the type of person or personality that your man is. Don't expect him to respond or be like someone else's man that might not be him. Don't compare. Celebrate the man that he is.
- **Know your man's cycle.** And act accordingly.
    - Know when he is chatty
    - Know when he needs to be left alone
- **Stop reacting to him.** Stop responding to the foolishness. Several years ago, I heard life coach

Paula White state:

"Speak to the King in him and not the foolish little boy that is acting out before you."

I believe this is so true. When you respond to the foolishness, it gets everyone off focus. To me, this is a universal truth for men and women. When dealing with a woman, speak to the queen in her and not the foolish little girl that is acting out before you. Bottom line: Stay in control and take the high road. At all cost.

- **Actions speak louder than words.** A man once told me he could not hear what I was saying because my guns were blazing, meaning I could not be heard past my attitude and my tone. He was so busy reacting to the attitude and tone in my voice, that he could not hear the words coming out of my mouth. Be sure when you are communicating in a fit of anger that your angry temperament is not drowning out your message.
- **Love on him.** Give him the attention that he craves. Trust me, it will be reciprocated.
- **Be his best friend.**
    - Encourage him
    - Motivate him
    - Cheer him on
- **Show off your man.** Edification is the best encourager.
- **Be a team player.** A man is a visionary. Be the partner that he needs to fulfill his vision.

- **Don't take him for granted.** We don't realize what we have until it's gone. Appreciate the person before you while you have the chance.
- **Pray for him.**

Encourage him. If you don't, who will? A man once told me that a woman has the power to teach a man how to treat her. Through her actions, she basically leaves a cookie-crumb trail for him to follow. Take the time to teach your man how to love you by loving him. I believe if you show love, you will receive love in return. I hope these tidbits will help in all of your relationships.

With love,

Judi

an We
Find
Love
Together?

MEN, WE AS WOMEN NEED YOU! Please know that relationships are not about us being right and you being wrong. They're not about us being super independent and not needing you. They're not about a woman doing better than a man financially, emotionally, or spiritually. It is not about any of this superficial nonsense. A REAL relationship is about what happens when the two forces known as male and female come together on an equal plane and explore friendship, commitment, authenticity, forgiveness, trust, and transparency. At the end of the day, that is what a relationship is about.

One of the biggest misconceptions and a major problem in relationships is the independent woman theory:

Women are viewed as not needing a man because they take care of everything for themselves.

This theory is so off-center, yet many women profess it and many men believe it. Let's dispel this theory: If a woman is single, then yes she is independent because she has to be. If a single woman doesn't work, pay the bills, etc., who will? Unlike a marriage where the man and woman are dependent on each other, single women **are independent out of a necessity; it comes with the territory.** Our independence does not mean that we emasculate your manhood. Our independence means that we are not lazy, trifling women, waiting to be rescued. We are women doing what needs to be done. And we are handling our business. Don't let our independence fool you. Please know that we want you, and more importantly, we need you.

According to some of the current societal perceptions, the only reason a woman needs a man is for certain projects and/or a sexual fix. Let me set the record straight: That is a LIE! That is NOT what we need from you. We need and desire you for so many reasons, some being:

- The companionship you bring
- The authority you possess
- The strength you nurture us with
- Your vulnerability that says you need us
- Your boyish charm
- Your take-charge demeanor
- Your ability to make us feel like we are the only woman on earth
- Your wisdom and the different perspective you bring
- The way you make me a better me because of you
- The wonderful us that we become when we are together
- Your stern correctness that helps us get back on the right path when we have strayed
- Your accountability
- Your partnership
- Your friendship
- Your love

Bottom line: WE NEED YOU! And YOU NEED US too!

With that being the case, what are we doing? Dignity, respect, morals, character, and integrity have fallen by the wayside. And for what? People are doing more now than ever in order to obtain a "false sense of companionship" or the "semblance of a relationship." And where has it gotten them? Nowhere. There are more lonely, miserable, dissatisfied, angry, bitter people than ever before; all because of the fear of being alone. There are a lot of GREAT men and women desiring and looking for love. And real love is attainable. However, some things need to be put in order.

Starting today, let's end the games, manipulation, and drama. Decide to want more from your relationships. Make a conscientious effort to use better judgment in choosing your mate. Realize that "**your type**" might not be right for you; the best looking, best dressed individual may not always be the "best" person for you. Stop making choices based on appearances and start choosing from your true heart's desire. Choose the one you need and the one that is right for you. I guarantee you will be much happier.

My prayer is that God brings the right person into your life. The one that was meant just for you!

Much love,

Judi

Please note: I cannot speak (and do not proclaim to speak) for every woman. However, I know quite a few women and have heard the concerns of many, so I speak on behalf of them as a group. Please hear their voices but more so, their hearts.

Are You Giving Your Haters Too Much Credit?

"LET YOUR HATERS BE YOUR MOTIVATORS" is a very common phrase and theme in today's pop culture. A hater is someone who is envious of someone else's success, drive, and/or ambition. Driven by jealousy, they attempt to tear down, destroy, or cast an aspersion on the other person's success.

In my humble opinion, I believe that we give too much credit to our haters. People who are focused enough to strive for their own personal greatness shouldn't take time out of their day to consider, talk about, or even acknowledge individuals that don't celebrate their accomplishments or their existence.

President Barack Obama was asked repeatedly in an interview with Barbara Walters about whether if Sarah Palin competed against him in the next presidential election, did he think that she would win. After delivering a very politically correct answer, Barbara Walters continued to press the issue and President Obama finally stated: "I don't think about Sarah Palin." Now to me, that was priceless! The president is trying to run the free world, and the last thing he needs to be concerned about is someone who is bitter that he won and she didn't.

I believe we should all take a lesson from President Obama and stay focused on the task at hand. A hater puts me in the mindset of a gnat—something that is an irritation that serves no necessary purpose. Don't allow your haters to distract you. Put them in their proper place and keep forging ahead. I have always been taught to go where you are celebrated and not where you are tolerated. I think that is excellent advice to follow.

As always, I wish you much success in every endeavor!

Much love,

Judi

Are You Destroying Your Relationships?

*W*OW, I REALLY BLEW IT! I had a run-in with a friend that caused so much anguish that it took several days to really address the situation. And did I ever! I went all out of my way to prove and get my point across. And after it was all said and done, I found out that in my need to be right and vindicated, I wounded a dear friend. In my pain, I did everything that I always share with everyone else not to do:

- Don't act on emotion
- Don't let your offense rule or dictate your actions
- Communicate—talk it out
- Don't make a permanent decision based on a temporary problem

Do you think I did any of that? Um, NO! In a later conversation, the person shared with me how much I hurt them and I could hear it in their voice; I just wanted to disappear. I was reminded at that moment that there are still two sides to every story and in spite of my pain, I owed a listening ear to their side. I never intended to hurt anyone; by the end of the conversation it was no longer about being right but how to salvage this relationship.

Now that the tension is subsiding, I dread the fact that I

didn't follow my own advice and I allowed my emotions to cloud my judgment. The relationship is on the mend and with time, it will grow stronger. Please learn from my mistakes. Don't allow your offense to cause you to act out of character. Avoid the self-inflicted chaos that I endured. Be led by this wise passage:

Do not be anxious about anything, but in everything, by prayer and petition, with thanksgiving, present your requests to God. And the peace of God, which transcends all understanding, will guard your hearts and your minds in Christ Jesus. Philippians 4:6-7 (NIV)

Now that's wisdom! You can't argue with truth!

Much success,

Judi

*I*N 2001 AFTER A DEVASTATING BETRAYAL, I was left severely wounded to the point of emotional paralysis. The pain from that betrayal was so severe and detrimental that I did not know how to process it. Although I had a good support system, I felt lost and alone. I honestly did not think that anyone around me could really comprehend the pain that I was feeling. While shopping at the grocery store, I passed a book kiosk and a colorful book cover caught my attention. It was as if this book was calling my name. When I read the title, I knew I had to have it. The title alone truly spoke to my pain. The book was *Just Enough Light for the Step That I'm On* by Stormie Omartian. At the time, I knew nothing about the book or the author, but I knew it contained the answers I needed.

In this book, Omartian shares the trials and tribulations of her childhood. As a result of her tumultuous experience, she was left with emotional baggage and scars. In each chapter, she shares her journey from victim to victor. I read the book as if it were my lifeline. Although our situations were different, there was still pain and the pain was real. Each chapter helped me take one step at a time toward my healing. The book contained healing scriptures that helped me to release my pain to the Lord. The chapters revealed someone who understood my pain as well as someone who had come out through the healing power of Jesus. Each chapter showed me how to do the same.

As the title states, sometimes we only have enough strength, enough faith, and enough courage for right now. What this book helped me to see was that I could walk out my healing, one step at a time. I didn't have to be the superhero, and I did not have to know all the answers. I just needed to take my time and allow the saving grace and the healing power of Jesus to help me reach my desired end, which was wholeness.

I think back on that book today, and the title still encourages me. So often we are overwhelmed and don't know which way to go or what to do. But if we would just take a moment from multitasking and take the pressure off of ourselves, we would be able to see that we have just enough light for the step we are CURRENTLY on. By taking one step at a time, we will find ourselves in a better place; a place of peace, joy, and tranquility.

If you are going through a difficult time or you are simply overwhelmed with the cares of life, free yourself and give yourself permission to take one step at a time.

Take time to allow the healing power of Jesus to deliver you and set you free.

Much love!

Judi

I CHALLENGE YOU TODAY to do something for someone else. We are so consumed with our own issues and drama that we forget to reach out and touch someone else. Even if only for one minute, take your eyes off of yourself and your problems and take a moment to help someone with theirs. Surprisingly, that minute will be worth more to you and be more beneficial than the 23 hours and 59 minutes remaining in your day.

You will find that when you divert your attention elsewhere, you gain better clarity on the situation at hand. Take time out to be the answer to someone else's prayer. I believe what you make happen for others, God will make that and more happen for you. Choose to sow love and reap a harvest of love, peace, and joy.

Spread the love!

Much love,

Judi

Your Pride Will Humble You

Humility is defined as the state or quality of being humble; absence of pride or self-assertion.

Humility can be a bad word to many, but an awesome blessing to those who choose to walk in it. I believe that God puts people in my life that force me to grow. He uses people who are a real thorn in my side; I refer to them as the unlovable—people who don't know how to apologize or admit they are wrong and constantly blame others. At times it seemed like I was always the one who had to humble myself and show the unconditional love of Christ and ask for forgiveness, even when I wasn't the one who initiated the drama. Needless to say after a few of these encounters, I'd had enough and I decided to have the "why me?" pity party. After I'd finish my very thorough venting session, God in His infinite wisdom had a few words to help me understand, "why me?":

God said:

> ***I loved you so much that I sent my only Son Jesus***
> ***to die for you. (John 3:16) But there are days***
> ***that I wait for you and you don't talk***
> ***to Me. The busyness of your day doesn't allow***
> ***you to pray and spend time with Me, like you***
> ***used to. Your priorities have changed. I am still***

the number one topic that you discuss but I am the last priority that you make time for. And how dare you not love My son or daughter. Yes, all of My children have issues, but so do you. And people deal with yours, why can't you deal with others? So humble yourself and walk in the unconditional love that I grant you and allow Me to use you for the glory of My Kingdom.

After I picked myself up off the floor from weeping and asking for forgiveness, I quickly forgot about the pride that I thought I had and completed the assignment at hand, which was to love the unlovable. In all honesty, it felt good.

I have learned that my preconceived notions (which are usually wrong) about a person or a situation causes my pride to rise up and makes the task harder than it is. In order to make my life easier, I have to get out of my own way. So let me help you, avoid the hot seat with God. The next time you second-guess walking in love and sharing the unconditional love of God, don't ask "why?" or "what about me?"; just think, "what about Him?" Allow God to guide you and to help you complete the task at hand. Your life will be so much richer.

What makes humility so desirable is the marvelous thing it does to us; it creates in us a capacity for the closest possible intimacy with God" —Monica Baldwin

Hugs,

Judi

Where Is the Love for Your Friends?

FRIENDSHIP IS A WONDERFUL THING. There is nothing like the love and commitment of a tried-and-true friend.

Recently I was reminded just how special and meaningful true friendship can be. I had the distinct pleasure of reconnecting with an old friend. We met for lunch at our favorite sushi restaurant, where we shared many laughs and war stories. Upon arrival, I was greeted with a huge smile accompanied with genuine joy and affection. This exchange was absolutely Priceless! After lunch, I had a smile on my face for the rest of the day. There is nothing like sharing with a real friend.

Although we lost contact and had not seen each other in more than a year, it was as if we had never skipped a beat. People come and go, but real friends remain. A friend to me is someone you can be vulnerable with by sharing your hopes, your dreams, and your fears. They are that special someone who won't judge you, but tells you the truth in love and challenges you to come up higher; someone who has your back and has your best interest at heart; someone who loves you in spite of you. A real friend holds your hand during bad times, celebrates with you in good times, and cries with you during sad times.

"Friends are born, not made." —Henry Adams

So often, we are so blinded by the day-to-day cares of life, that we forget about those special people in our lives called friends. We might not talk to them every day but they are there. We might not spend time with them like we used to but they are still there. And when we think that our world has caved in on us and we are all alone, they are right there. We all have people who are special to us; but we may have lost contact with them or just don't have the freedom to spend time with them as often as we like. However, when it's all said and done, they are waiting in the wings with open arms ready to just be your friend.

Take a moment to enjoy and celebrate those special people in your life called friends. Give them a call. Share the love.

Love,

Judi

"It is not your business how someone treats you. It is your business how you treat someone. You treat people the way you want to be treated. Remember you will reap what you sow. If you are so busy focused on what someone else is doing you are missing your blessing by not focusing on what you should be doing. What seeds are you sowing?"—Creflo Dollar

As you can imagine, that was a **BITTER** pill to swallow. As human beings, we are reactionary. The human creed is whatever you do to me, I will do to you. However, as Christians, we are to turn the other cheek when we have been wronged and walk in the love of Jesus Christ with others, especially those who are not as loving or kind. This love walk is not easy. It took me a while to process the words of Creflo Dollar. The more I thought about it, the more I realized they were true. If I am sharing and showing the love of Christ with people, especially to those who have wronged me, God will convict them and hopefully change will occur; that is God's business, not mine.

I have learned that God does things in His own time and although His time is not my time, He will still handle it. Me, on the other hand, I want God to handle it right then and there and if He doesn't handle it in the timely manner that I deem adequate, I feel the need to help Him. After years of growing with God, I have learned the hard way; that He doesn't need my help and He can handle it so much better without me. I realized that the desired change will not happen if we are constantly in the way trying to assist God. God doesn't need our help. God needs our obedience and submission.

Dear friends, don't take revenge. Let God fight your battle. He handles the situation so much better than you ever could. I will admit this passage is a hard one to swallow, but it is full of wisdom and truth:

> *Don't hit back; discover beauty in everyone. If you've got it in you, get along with everybody. Don't insist on getting even; that's not for you to do. "I'll do the judging," says God. "I'll take care of it." Our Scriptures tell us that if you see your enemy hungry, go buy that person lunch, or if he's thirsty, get him a drink. Your generosity will surprise him with goodness. Don't let evil get the best of you; get the best of evil by doing good.*
> *Romans 12:19-21 (The Message)*

I know it's hard, but be encouraged! Continue to walk in the love of Christ and allow the Lord to fight your battles. I promise He will do a much better job than you. Here is to OUR growth!

Much love,

Judi

Love and Encouragement Challenge

An OLD FRIEND FOUND ME ON FACEBOOK, and as he read my information tab, he was so excited about the various endeavors I'm pursuing that he picked up the phone to share his support and encouragement. I can't begin to tell you how that made my day. I don't think I stopped smiling the entire day. Sometimes we just need a random act of kindness to encourage us on our journey. A little appreciation goes a long way.

I would like to challenge you to encourage others on their journeys. Starting today, make an effort to reach out to not only those in your immediate circle, but to old friends that you have lost contact with, co-workers, associates, and even strangers. Let them know how much you appreciate them. Let them know you care. Show them some love and encourage them in their endeavors.

Are you up for the challenge? I am! Let me be the first to show my appreciation.

I would like to thank each of you for purchasing this book. Your support encourages me to continue writing. My prayer is that this book is a blessing to you. May the words offer helpful insight and may they touch your life in a meaningful way. ♥

See, it is just that easy. Now it is your turn to show some love.

With love,

Judi

Finding Love Outside the Box

You NEVER LOSE BY LOVING. You always lose by holding back.— Barbara De Angelis

I must admit I am a romantic at heart and at the same time, a realist. So I truly believe in love. I also believe (and have experienced) that you can have the wish list of potential mates that fit "my type," yet end up loving someone who is totally opposite of what you wanted or expected. The old adage is true— *love is blind*. I believe that is one of many reasons why there seems to be an increase in women dating younger men. I am sure a majority of these women would prefer to date someone closer to their age, but I believe they are relieved that they ventured out past their comfort zone.

I can certainly understand the attraction to a younger man, because lately I've noticed a lot of younger men really have their acts together. Some of the men that I have met in passing have been very grounded, focused, goal-oriented visionaries, who are serious about the direction of their lives. Many also desire a committed relationship that leads to marriage. While dining with friends, I met such a man, who happened to be our waiter. After exchanging the initial pleasantries, we discovered that we all had common interests, which opened the door to further conversation. He shared stories with us about his dreams, aspirations, and his girlfriend. When asked if she was the one, shaking his head emphatically, YES! He stated:

"Most definitely. We have been in this relationship for six years. I am not going to let anyone else get her. I am vested."

Our conversation revealed that his girlfriend is 6'2" and I would venture to say that our waiter was maybe 5'6". Initially the height difference might throw you, but after talking with him throughout the night, we could see how the height difference would not even be an issue. Our waiter was very confident, charming, goal-oriented, and full of personality. His attentiveness was laudable. Now I am sure that you would say, of course, he was your waiter, that is what he is supposed to do.

Initially, he wasn't our waiter. Due to a mix-up, we were seated in his section by mistake and once realized, he assisted in moving us to our original table. His demeanor, caring attitude, and personality caused us to request his service. Throughout the night, we laughed and joked as if we were old friends. His transparency and honesty were very refreshing. In the end, he earned more than just a tip; he earned our respect and accolades.

This is not an isolated incident. But this exchange, coupled with many others, have made me really step back and gain a new perspective on dating outside of your "comfort zone." Based on my most recent experiences, I can see why women have a very strong attraction to younger men. However it comes with a price: Understanding that when you deviate away from the norm, your decisions come with repercussions of the masses, disapproving looks, stares, and judgment of others, especially your peers. Despite the opinions of others, you have to choose to live your life for you and do what is going to make you happy.

It really makes you wonder what wonderful life experiences you've missed out on fearing the opinion of others.

Thinking back to the waiter, I can only imagine the looks of disbelief when people see this significantly "height-challenged" couple. No matter what others think, they are happy and that is all that matters. I believe as human beings, we are so careful to consider the opinions of others that we stifle our own happiness and existence. You can't allow the opinion of others to dictate your happiness, or you will never be happy. Only you can determine what makes you happy. So allow yourself the pleasure and freedom of loving someone who might not be your "traditional type." Make the choice that is best for you and choose to be HAPPY! **At the end of the day, YOUR happiness can only be determined by YOU!**

Here is to your liberation and freedom in every area of your life! Set your OWN personal standards for your life! I hope my epiphany has helped you gain a new perspective, be it in love or life. We only have one life to live, so live it to the fullest!

Much love,

Judi

Disclaimer: I love and respect ALL men. Although this highlights younger men, I believe that all men, no matter the age, have wonderful characteristics that are worth celebrating. So I salute you all!

Prescription for Mental Peace?

Recently, a dear friend contacted me, extremely upset, regarding matters of the heart. As the details were shared, I noticed that assumptions and accusations were beginning to appear in the midst of the story. When asked if the accusations had been substantiated, I received the following answer:

"No, but I know them and I know that is what they are plotting and scheming…"

I think we all know that scenario all too well. A familiar scene when someone has been wounded by a loved one. The hurt and pain of betrayal causes our minds to create very colorful scenarios as to how we ended up in this predicament. We don't know if our self-concocted scenarios are true, but we convince ourselves that they are and from there, an emotional explosion erupts. Once the truth is finally revealed, the feeling of shame and embarrassment is prevalent; to think that we allowed our minds to go down such a wrong path is reprehensible. Then there is the physical drain from the emotional roller coaster of assumption, presumption, or whatever "umption" you want to call it, that will leave you spent and burned out.

Several years ago, I heard someone speak on the law of belief. The premise of the law of belief:

Whatever you believe with feeling becomes your reality.

The question that followed caused me to pause:

What do you actually believe that ISN'T real but has become your reality?

Instantly, I thought about my conversation with my friend. In addition, I thought back to the times I created my own crazy scenarios that were so far from the truth. I then begin to realize how much time and energy I had wasted on a false reality caused by emotionalism. I was left speechless.

Life experiences, such as these continue to bring more validity to the words, **Free Your Mind**. With so much wasted time and emotional energy, I have reminded myself to look at situations from a different perspective. I have to change my viewpoint as well as my response and create my own mental peace through the following actions:

- Take time to calm down
- Don't act on emotions
- Evaluate your perception—Do I have the right outlook on the situation?
- Choose to seek truth, not assumptions or accusations

I believe this prescription for mental peace will lead you to the place where the truth and tranquility you seek awaits; a place where you are in control of yourself, your emotions, and the situation at hand. You will no longer feel the stress or emotional pull of the circumstances; instead you will find yourself trusting God to handle the situation for you. My prayer is that the peace of God will guard your heart and mind.

With love,

Judi

EAR LADIES:

In my travels, I have encountered a number of women (too many actually) that have expressed pain, regret, and discontentment regarding their relationships. Out of desperation, these women have done things in an effort to keep a man who didn't want to be kept. In their minds, having half of a man is better than no man at all. Why are so many women choosing to settle when it comes to a man?

Women are constantly being bombarded by the media, friends, and well meaning strangers on how to find, keep, and marry a man. But nowhere in these self-help trilogies are women admonished to have self-respect and dignity in the pursuit of love. The focus is solely on a woman satisfying a man, mentally, physically, and sexually. This consistent message, coupled with the lie that there are only a few good single men left, has caused some women to lower their standards and do whatever it takes to keep a man; and these choices have caused a lot of women to be miserable in their relationships.

The top complaints that I've heard from women are:

1. He doesn't love me
2. He doesn't respect me

3. I can't keep him
4. I want my own man

Let's address each of these complaints one at a time.

He doesn't love me:

When I hear this statement, I always have a few questions to ask: Did he say he loved you? If he didn't state that he loved you, why do you have expectations that he did? Did he deserve your love? Did he earn your love? Did you throw your love freely his way? Most of the time, the answer is that he did not earn your love. In that case, anyone will take something that is free. If you don't put demands, restrictions, or parameters around your heart, it will be taken for granted. Remember, you are a precious jewel and everyone can't see your worth or your value. But those who are worthy of you will recognize who and what you are.

Take your time. Allow yourself to get to know people and let them earn the right to your heart. If you want to stop the hurt and the pain, make a decision to stop throwing your heart away to anyone and everyone. You deserve better.

He doesn't respect me:

My question is: Do you respect yourself? Let me share with you what men are saying. I heard a 30-year-old male colleague state:

"It's a shame when a man has more respect for a woman than a woman has for herself."

I have heard other men state:

"Women give of themselves sexually too easily."

"In a new relationship, women should not have sex for at least 90 days, if that".

"Men really prefer a woman not to have sex with them. It keeps the chase going. Don't get me wrong, I will have sex with her, but I would prefer her to say no."

It is a sad day when a man has to tell a woman not to have sex or not to have sex too soon. Ladies, do you demand respect? Do you behave in an unladylike manner? Do you find yourself in precarious situations that you are ashamed of? Do you allow a man to speak to you in a disrespectful manner? Does he refer to you with terms like "B" or a "whore"? Is the answer to any of these questions, yes? If so, **WHY**? Do you think that this will help you get or keep a man? It won't. **Please don't ever disrespect yourself for anyone.** When you respect yourself, others will respect you. Always remember, your actions teach people how to treat you and they will follow your lead accordingly. Decide today to respect yourself and others will do the same. Demand respect and you will be respected!

I can't keep a man:

This is a hard one, but let's start with this question: Was he yours in the first place? I know this is a harsh question, but some women are extremely guilty of fantasizing about a relationship and making it more than what it is. Here is a plain and very simple example: Just because he said you look nice doesn't mean he is madly in love with you. He only meant that you looked nice. And that's it! Nothing more!

I am a firm believer that if a man wants you, he will tell you. You won't have to figure it out, decode his conversations, or interrogate your friends for their relationship analyses. And when a man tells you he doesn't want you, he means it. He doesn't want you. So no matter how much you do for him or how much sex you have with him, he will still not be your man. It goes back to respect. If you are giving a man the "world" for free with no demands or stipulations, he will take it. It doesn't mean he is in love with you. It just means that he was just along for the ride. Ladies, make sure that the effort that you are putting forth towards this relationship is being reciprocated by your potential mate. It should be an equal balance of give and take.

Most importantly, be sure that the man you are trying to keep wants to be kept, and then make sure that he wants to be kept by you.

I want my own man:

Don't we all. And the best way to get your man is to love yourself, respect yourself, and enjoy yourself. Do you! When you are busy taking care of you, you will be found. Too often, women are obsessing about a man, getting one, keeping one, or replacing one. Instead spend that energy and time on you. Pursuing your destiny and fulfilling your God-given purpose. And while you are focused on you and enjoying your life—your man—the right man will come.

I interviewed a variety of men ages 25 to 55 and asked what they found sexy or appealing about a woman, and the answers were all the same:

- Intelligent
- Confident: a woman who knows her value and worth

- Friendly, outgoing, fun loving
- Clothing: fashionable, but leaves something to the imagination
- A woman who takes care of herself: hair, nails, etc.
- A woman that challenges a man to be the best he can be

Of course, opinions will vary. But at the end of the day, you want a man who wants you, loves you, and wants to see you succeed. **PLEASE DON'T SETTLE.** There is a great man waiting just for you, one who is worthy of you and you worthy of him. Wait for him.

It really grieves me to constantly hear the horror stories from women regarding relationships that have gone wrong. We all have experienced the hurt, pain, and devastation from making poor choices. But don't let that pain go in vain. Pick up the pieces, learn from those mistakes, and make a vow to put yourself first, to love yourself, respect yourself, and to demand the best for yourself. I truly believe that you will see a difference in not only the caliber of men you attract, but the person that you will become.

I wish you nothing but God's best in every area of your life.

Much love,

Judi

Please note: This is not intended to be offensive. It is meant as a wake-up call. Although it is directed toward women, it applies to men as well. Please receive it in the loving concern in which it was sent.

Are You Choosing Wisely?

I WILL BE THE FIRST TO ADMIT, I had no desire to see the movie *For Colored Girls*, Tyler Perry's rendition of Ntozake Shange's play, *For Colored Girls Who Have Considered Suicide When the Rainbow is Enuf*. For me, the title of the play was enough to deter my desire. This was definitely not a topic that I wanted to deal with as a source of entertainment. But for whatever reason, something kept pulling me to see this movie and I can honestly say I was not prepared for the intensity and grittiness that the movie contained.

However painful to watch, *For Colored Girls* was a harsh reality check of what some people are enduring in life and in their relationships. It really put a face to the stories that we hear from coworkers, relatives, and even friends. Although the movie is entitled *For Colored Girls*, I really wish that Tyler Perry would have used an array of ethnicities and cultures because the subject matter is not only experienced by women of color, but by all women. I understand why he didn't in an effort to stay true to the material, but this is a movie that reaches far beyond color lines. There is a woman in every culture and socioeconomic position enduring what these women endured and even more. I believe this is a must see-movie for men and women in an effort to really understand what some women have endured as well as to gain a better understanding of their pain.

Despite the grittiness of the film, I am so glad that the overwhelming theme of choices and their consequences was highlighted. The fact that these were all CHOICES that these women made, whether they were good or bad, or whether the actions did or did not warrant the given responses, it still all boiled down to choices. It was a very harsh reminder that our choices can sometimes have very cruel consequences. I hope that this movie will cause a dialog between women as well as men and women in their relationships. After viewing *For Colored Girls,* I hope that women will begin to re-evaluate their relationship decisions. It took me several days after the movie to determine if I even liked it or not. I was so consumed with the ugly sound of truth from the movie ringing in my head, I could not help but wonder if I could have been (or had been) one of those women, but with different results.

Just by reviewing the scenarios, I wondered, for instance, if I had been:

- Too trusting
- Too naive and ignored the truth that was before me
- Too optimistic for change to occur
- Wanting love so badly that I avoided the pain of loneliness by convincing myself to stay

We have all made mistakes in the name of love or companionship. Any of us could have been one or all of these women. It really just boils down to whether we chose to be or not.

If we learn nothing else from this movie, let's learn to make the RIGHT choices to achieve the results we desire. You only have one life. Live it to the fullest and enjoy every moment. But in doing so, choose wisely. And most of all, **LOVE YOURSELF to the fullest before you try to love someone else. Always be true to you!**

Written with much love,

Judi

Are You Guilty of the "Just In Case" Syndrome?

*I*T'S TIME FOR TRUE CONFESSIONS...

Thanksgiving week 2010 was an interesting one to say the least. It had been a week full of letting go of the old and making room for the new. One afternoon, a friend who is a professional organizer had recently taken me on as a client, and the first step was to conduct a clothing inventory of my closet. This was just the first phase of the process. We examined every piece of clothing I own. We discussed each item, the look that I am trying to achieve, and the variations that my garments could be worn in. After a thorough review, each item was placed in one of four categories:

1. Give away—e.g. Goodwill
2. Resale—Consignment shop
3. Maybe—could possibly keep but it was up for discussion
4. Winner—I could keep

HEAR ME when I say that this process was more painful than I thought it would be. We all have some items that we know have to go, and for the most part, we are okay with that. But others, we keep for various reasons such as the cost factor or it's one of our favorite pieces. And then there are those few items we forget they existed.

As we began skimming down my wardrobe, I REALLY began to comprehend the **theme of the mission: YOUR OLD STUFF HAS GOT TO GO!**

I noticed that my tone turned from jovial to defiant. At first it began with an upbeat, *"I know you are going to make me give this away"* (LOL) to a defiant *"I am keeping this!"* It almost came down to a battle of wills and my friend finally had to say to me, *"Well, if you are going to tell me what you are going to keep, then why am I here?"* Although it was all done in jest, we both meant what we said and stood our grounds. As a self-professed pack rat going through this process, I realized that we don't recognize how attached we are to some things until we have to let them go. And then we begin to have a war with ourselves justifying their purpose, while simultaneously, the reality of the truth is revealed. My turning point occurred when she said these awful words to me:

"When was the last time you wore this?" OUCH! Did you hear that? That was the sound of my feet being stepped on. Do you know how bad that hurt? OMGosh! Really? Did you have to take it there? There it was staring me in the face, the reality that I had to face. The burden was then put on me to ask myself:

Why are you holding on to something that no longer serves a purpose in your life?

Needless to say, she won with that point. Three hours and four HUGE trash bags later, we completed phase one of the closet inventory. Phase two would consist of downsizing even more. Geez…

After she left, since I was still in inventory mode, I mentally switched from clothing to people. I began to think about an associate who seemed to want to hold on; I refer to these types of people as stragglers. You know those associates or former friends whose time has come and gone in your life, but they linger around just in case they need you, so they can have access to you. As I began to evaluate the situation, I had to be honest with myself and acknowledge the part that I played in this dragged-out association. Deep within, I wanted to believe the best regarding this individual, so I allowed access, believing for change. But in the end, the truth is the truth: If it walks, talks, quacks, and acts like a duck, it's a duck. So I had to make sure that I put myself where I needed to be, out of harm's way. It was time to end this association. I remained cautious to stay in the vein that I was in and truly sever that connection. In doing so, I felt the peace that was long overdue from this confusing tango.

As you can imagine, I was feeling pretty good. I had de-cluttered my closet and my group of associates. I was excited for the holiday festivities to begin. Then on Thursday, yes Thanksgiving Day, the straggler saga continued. As the Happy Thanksgiving phone calls and text messages rolled in, I received a text from an ex who knows and understands why he is an ex; since we have two separate agendas, there was no need to reply. I don't know if this was a week of testing or self-evaluation but you can believe I was taking heed to the lessons. This series of events reminded me of a friend's post on Facebook that stated: ***I am getting rid of the "just in case."*** He was referring to the stuff that we hold onto "just in case" we need it someday, and that day never comes.

I realized that a lot of times, we hold onto people, clothes, etc, just in case we need them. But what we don't realize is while those people and/or things are in our lives, they are hindering the entrance of the new person, place, or thing that God has in store for us. The old adage is true; you can't receive anything new if your hand is full. From people to clothing, the lesson is the same. Although their season in your life has come to an end, it does not negate that they served a purpose. By the same token, the realization that their purpose has been served and their services are no longer needed must be acknowledged.

Be honest with yourself and conduct a life inventory. Begin to evaluate whoever or whatever has expired in your life, and put it in its proper place. Set it free so that someone else can benefit from it. Remove the stragglers in your life who don't bring you joy and peace. Stop entertaining a conversation with someone whose relationship you no longer cherish, and be selfless by setting them free to find the person who will.

I pray that God gives you the strength and peace to make the decisions that you need to make to rid yourself of the "just in case."

Much love,

Judi

Bring Closure to a Relationship

I RECENTLY ATTENDED A PARTY and joined a group discussion already in progress. A young lady shared a story regarding the end of a valued friendship. She agreed that they both had a few issues to work through, but at the same time, she thought that they were in "friendship time out." The friend made a request via email that let the other know in no uncertain terms that their friendship had ended. She reached out to the young lady via phone, but no response. She eventually complied with the email request and was left hanging in the wings. Hurt and devastated, she replayed the scenario over in her mind. What happened? How did their friendship get to this point? Why is it so easy for her to walk away from our friendship? In the end, she never received the closure that she was looking for or felt she deserved.

This scenario brings up a good point: How do you end a relationship? Be it platonic or intimate, it is never easy to let go of someone that you care about or who has been an integral part of your life. Sometimes relationships end due to a disagreement or unresolved problems. But more often than not, if we are honest with ourselves, the relationship ended long before the disagreement occurred. Most of the time, the real issue is that the individuals involved have grown apart.

Each person is on a different path and no one really knows how to handle the situation. So it is usually avoided like the plague, and if the situation is finally addressed, it comes out in an argument. A heated battle ensues that turns ugly where words are spoken that should not have been; feelings are hurt and something that was once beautiful is now a painful disaster.

I recently polled a group of adults between the ages of 25 and 55 and asked, "How do you end a relationship?" Sad to say, the majority of those polled stated that they would:

- Just stop talking to the person
- Stop taking their phone calls, ignore text messages or emails
- Just shut them off completely

The poll results left me speechless. I polled adults, not children. When the group was asked if the situation were reversed, would they want closure? Overwhelmingly the answer was YES. Now, where is the balance? How do you expect to receive something you are not willing to give? It is amazing how so many people want closure but are unwilling to offer it to others. The idea of handling your friendships like a 4-year-old child who takes his toys and goes home is absurd. By the result of this poll, it is apparent that it is time for the grownups to grow up.

If you or someone you know is having problems communicating the end of a relationship, maybe the following will help create the needed closure.

Steps to creating closure:

- Reach out to the individual(s) and set aside a time to sit down and talk
- Address the problem(s)
- Acknowledge the issues and work through them one by one
- Address your expectations and your unmet needs of your friendship
- Acknowledge your participation in the situation; in most situations, not just one person is to blame
- Confront the fact that maybe they did you wrong, but in the end you allowed them to
- Come prepared to be open and honest and ready to give and receive what is put on the table
- Remember you can only be responsible for you

The purpose of the meeting is to offer each participant an opportunity to share his/her viewpoint and bring closure to the relationship. You will not always agree. But respect each person's individual point of view. Most people would rather act as the group polled and disappear than confront the situation. Although many avoid closure, it offers a variety of benefits that aid in your individual development.

Closure allows for the following to occur:

- An understanding of the other person's point of view
- How others perceive you and your actions
- Fosters growth
- Forces individuals to become better communicators
- Each participant leaves with an understanding of why

the friendship ended
- Allows individuals to learn how to become a better person and a better friend, which is the most important element in the end

It is never easy to see a friendship come to an end. However, with as much energy and effort that you put in the friendship to maintain it, should you not also do the same to end it? Closure is important; be sure to treat people the way you want to be treated.

Love,

Judi

I WROTE *THE CHLOE CHRONICLES: LIFE LESSONS I LEARNED FROM MY COCKER SPANIEL,* THE FIRST BOOK IN THIS SERIES. My dog Chloe was a special dog that lived by her own set of rules. Just by her actions she became a four-legged life coach to everyone she encountered. Chloe taught me how to live, love, and just enjoy life to the fullest and through the following lessons, I hope she will inspire you to do the same.

I give you… the Chloe Mantra:

- Love unconditionally!
- Forgive immediately!
- Attempt to rectify an error or mistake instantly.
- Let go of an offense: IT'S NOT WORTH IT!!!!
- Play with those who want to play with you. Walk away from those who don't.
- Realize you can't force anyone to like or love you. If they are unable to see your worth, then they are obviously not worthy of you.
- Believe you are special! You are valuable! You are worthy! Accept it! Embrace it! Walk in it!
- Most of all, know that you are loved.
- Sow love and you will reap love.

I believe those are pretty good rules to live by. Much Success.

With love,

Judi

Conclusion

Thank you for allowing me to share my heart. My prayer and sincere desire is that you were able to learn from my mistakes and avoid all of the wasted time, energy, and resources that I endured.

Remember, give and require what you want in a relationship and most importantly, set realistic expectations. I'm pretty sure you will see the results you desire.

"A friend is someone who knows all about you and loves you just the same"—Elbert Hubbard

I don't think that it can get any better than that. I believe the love that we seek for self and with others is strengthen by the love that is mentioned in the bible. As a Christian, I've found that the greatest love of all is that of Jesus Christ. If you are interested in finding out more information about the unconditional love of Jesus Christ or the Christian faith, feel free to visit: www.judimason.com/faith

As always, this has been written in love.

From my heart with love,

Judi

Thanks so much for your support. I hope you have enjoyed *The Relationship Chronicles*, the second installment of the three-part *Chronicle* series, which also includes *The Chloe Chronicles: Life Lessons I Learned from My Cocker Spaniel*, and the third installment, *The Best Self Chronicles: Discovering Your Authentic Self*, due out fall 2012. Be sure to pick up your copies!

Let's stay connected via social media:

Be sure to visit my blog and add your name to my email list to stay abreast of the latest happenings. Just sign up on my website: www.judimason.com

Follow Me on…

Twitter: twitter.com/judimason

Facebook: facebook.com/judimason.empowerment

Have a question? Email me at: judi@divaink.com

From my heart:

I really want you to become the BEST YOU that you can be. Make every day count and choose to live on purpose.
Let's make YOUR DREAMS become a reality!

Much love,

Judi

Empowered to Empower Others!

www.ingramcontent.com/pod-product-compliance
Lightning Source LLC
LaVergne TN
LVHW041628070426
835507LV00008B/510